GROWING UP JEWISH

or

Why Is This Book Different

From All Other Books?

ב"ה

RABBI JACK MOLINE

To An Uncommon Bibliographical Expert:

Illustrations by Marcia Simha

August, 5748

Dear David,
  Birthdays
  Are   ...May yours be
  Rarely   a collector's item!
  Observed
  Nowadays ... **PENGUIN BOOKS** מזל|ה פו| nNe
                                        Joey

PENGUIN BOOKS
Viking Penguin Inc., 40 West 23rd Street,
New York, New York 10010, U.S.A.
Penguin Books Ltd, Harmondsworth,
Middlesex, England
Penguin Books Australia Ltd, Ringwood,
Victoria, Australia
Penguin Books Canada Limited, 2801 John Street,
Markham, Ontario, Canada L3R 1B4
Penguin Books (N.Z.) Ltd, 182-190 Wairau Road,
Auckland 10, New Zealand

First published in Penguin Books 1987
Published simultaneously in Canada

A ^{2}**M** COMMUNICATIONS PRODUCTION

"The Yuppie Haggadah" first appeared in the *Baltimore Jewish Times*.
Portions of "The Jewish Calendar for Today" first appeared in *Times
Outlook* as "A Gentile's Highly Inaccurate Guide to Jewish Holidays."
Portions of "TV Listings" first appeared in *Sh'ma* magazine as "Shushan
Television Programs."

Library of Congress Cataloging in Publication Data
Moline, Jack.
   Growing up Jewish, or Why is this book different from
all other books?
      1. Judaism—Anecdotes, facetiae, satire, etc.
2. Youth, Jewish—United States—Anecdotes, facetiae,
satire, etc.   3. Jewish wit and humor. I. Title.
II. Title: Growing up Jewish.   III. Title: Why is this
book different from all other books?
BM582.M65   1987   296   87-7606
ISBN 0-14-009836-4

Printed in the United States of America by
R.R. Donnelley & Sons Company,
Harrisonburg, Virginia
Set in Franklin Gothic Book
Design: VIRGINIA RUBEL

To everybody in the world except Danny Siegel

CONTENTS

Introduction

Why is this book different from all other books?
  Well, first of all, I wrote it. At least most of it.
  Second, it is funny. At least most of it.
  And third, it is the real truth. At least some of it.
  Actually, to be authentic, I ought to have four answers. So here is the only intentionally serious thing in the whole book.

My generation shuttled between urban apartments and suburban developments, between Little League and Hebrew School, between Daddy's parents for first seder and Mommy's for second seder (after all, that's why there are two, right?). We knew the "old world" through our grandparents and their friends, who taught us creative ways to wreak havoc with the English language. We also knew the comforts of their homes and rituals. We knew the American dream through split-level synagogues and upward mobility. We knew the modern world through Vietnam, rock 'n' roll, and the Jetsons. There was so much to enjoy, and so much laughter.

I didn't write a primer on Judaism, nor an attack on religion and tradition. I wrote about what I love, what I love so much that it doesn't matter to me whether you are laughing at me or with me—or not at all, for that matter—as long as the book is bought and paid for.

If you are offended, write to me. I won't answer, but you'll feel better. If you are inspired, send me your inspirations. Maybe they'll wind up in Volume II. If you don't understand the book, chances you (a) are not Jewish, (b) never spend much time in a Jewish community, or (c) se habla espanol. I suggest you buy a bagel, a bottle of Schapiro's Extra-Heavy Sacramental Concord Wine, and a Billy Crystal album, and then reread the book.

Enough already. Turn the page, and you're on your way to understanding what makes a Jew tick, other than a Middle-Eastern terrorist.

Don't worry, the rest of the book is funnier.

—RABBI JACK MOLINE
Purim 5747

GENESIS

FIRST THINGS FIRST

The Qumran Parchment

In 1952, while excavating some ruins at a site along the Dead Sea known as Qumran a-Mara Thon, archaeologists discovered a rolled parchment containing a remarkable version of the first book of the Bible. Scholars had long known that numerous versions of the Bible existed prior to the canonization of our standard text in the second century C.E. This, however, was their first look at such a version and it was quite a Revelation.

Scientists date the scroll to the second century B.C.E. and have hypothesized that it was an official text of the Essenes, or Hebraic sect of Heavy Eaters. The Essenes may have been the first to elevate heartburn into a Jewish religious symbol. Judging from the text, they also adhered to the doctrine of Divine Fallibility, the belief that "if God did not exist, He would have no one to blame but Himself."

No further introduction is necessary. The significance of this scroll can be grasped by even the most unsophisticated reader, someone like yourself. Here, then, are selections from *Bereishith*, or Genesis, the first of the Five Books of Moses.

> *In the beginning the Lord God, Who erreth infrequently, though when He does it is a whopper, created the heavens and the earth, and divided the firmament, saying, "Let there be light." And He saw the light, that it was good, or at least better than the darkness for reading.*

...and man became evil and corrupt. But Noah walked with God and begot three sons, Ham, Cheese, and Curly. Later, Curly was replaced with Shem, but it was never quite the same.

...and Shem begot Joe. And Joe begot Curly Joe. And Curly Joe begot Terach. And Terach begot Abraham, but by then the act had fallen apart. And Abraham was one hundred years old when his son Isaac was born. And the Lord came to Abraham, telling him to take his son to Mount Moriah, where Isaac would die. And Abraham replied, "Of course he'll die on Moriah. Let him play the Nevele first—it's an easier crowd."

And Isaac wed Rebecca, who bore him twin sons, Esau and Jacob. And Jacob connived Esau out of his birthright, cheated him out of Isaac's blessing, and deceived his father.

And Jacob was a man of the Lord.

And Jacob wed Leah. And Rachel. And Bilhah. And Zilpah. And he went to them frequently, for Jacob was not only a man of the Lord, he was also a man of the Ladies. And Leah, Bilhah, and Zilpah each conceived and bore Jacob many sons; but Rachel was barren. And God remembered Rachel and finally she too bore a child, and they called him Joseph. And Jacob loved Joseph more than all his children, and gave him his many-colored raccoon coat from college days.

But Joseph's brothers conspired against him and sold him to a band of Ishmaelites going to Egypt for a gig. And Judah showed Jacob the raccoon coat, which the brothers had dipped in goat blood, and said, "Thy son was devoured by an aggravated dromedary." And Jacob responded, "Where is said dromedary, I wish to see that which hath devoured my son." And Judah said, "About a mile off." And Jacob walked the mile for the camel, but found it not. In anguish, he rent his garments, fortunately making enough for a new raccoon coat.

. . . and it came to pass at the end of two years that the great Pharoah of Egypt had a series of upsetting dreams. And Pharoah, hearing that the Hebrew Joseph could interpret dreams, had him brought from the dungeon. And Joseph explained to Pharoah that there would be seven good years followed by seven years of famine, but that proper planning, under the management of a Hebrew dream-interpreter, could avert disaster.

And Pharoah was so pleased that he appointed Joseph to the post and renamed him Zaphenathpaneah, explaining, "I don't know, he just looks like a Zaphenathpaneah."

And it came to pass that Joseph's predictions came true. And no one was more surprised than Joseph. And the famine was all over the earth; and all the countries came to Joseph to buy corn. And among the buyers were Joseph's brothers, who knew him not, though he knew them. And after a few fun-laden pranks involving bondage, kidnapping, and threats of fratricide, Joseph revealed his true identity and invited the family to spend the weekend.

And Jacob and his clan came to Egypt. And Jacob, upon seeing Joseph alive, exclaimed, "Now I may die since I have seen thy face." And Joseph was a wee bit insulted, for he hadn't thought he looked that bad.

And God heeded Jacob's wish and let him die, seventeen years later. And his sons carried him back to Canaan and buried him in the cave of Macherplace.

. . . and Joseph lived a scant hundred and ten years and was buried in Egypt.

Circumcision: The Penile Code

From the time of Abraham, Jews have been commanded to cut the foreskin off the penis of every eight-day-old baby boy, as well as every male convert. This seems to be the most solid evidence yet that God Almighty is a woman with a perverse sense of humor.

Nonetheless, the *brit milah* (covenant of the circumcision) or "briss" as it is known colloquially, is a time of great rejoicing. At a time when pride in tradition is blending with modern values, circumcision has become a sort of nose job you wear in your pants.

The surgery is performed by a specially trained circumcision expert, called a *mohel* (sometimes pronounced *moyl*) with the clamps and knives known as the "briss kit." (Hence, the custom of serving roast beef after the ceremony.)

Truth be told, the fear of losing that little piece of unnecessary skin has prevented Judaism from gaining its share of converts. How many times has a Rabbi, explaining the beauty of tradition to a rapt listener, concluded with, ". . . and then all you have to do is cut off the end of your penis . . ." only to see the potential convert closing the office door behind him.

New studies have shown, however, that the benefits of circumcision outweigh by far the losses. Researchers have discovered that a hormone which makes people stupid is manufactured exclusively in the foreskin of the penis. According to the report of this decade-long study, every single man who was circumcised "was smart enough never to do that again."

Once again, the Bible's wisdom is vindicated.

Hebrew School: The Jewish Alternative to Little League

Everyone agrees that there are few places children would like to be less after a full day of school than sitting in a classroom learning a foreign language. Nevertheless, from the age of six Jewish children dutifully trudge off to Hebrew School anywhere from one to six days a week to learn about Jewish holidays, Jewish history, and Hebrew.

Ah, Hebrew, ancient language reborn. In Hebrew School children learn to do two things: read phonetically aloud so that they can make it through their Bar Mitzvah without embarrassment, and sing Israeli songs so they can join in the fun when they visit the homeland.

The trouble is, no one ever bothered to explain the meanings of the songs. Take as an example, *"Tzeina, Tzeina."* It's peppy, its words have enough guttural sounds to impress the family that it's really in Hebrew, and it is universally recognized. But what does it mean?

Go out, go out, go out, go out,
Jewish daughters, and see
The soldiers on the collective settlement.
Do not, do not, do not, do not,
Do not be afraid
Of a soldier, a member of the army.

Many Jewish girls have gone to Israel and heeded this advice, succumbing to the subliminal suggestions planted by years of Hebrew School assemblies and parents' programs. Oh well, at least he's Jewish.

Or how about "*Zum gali gali*"? This song is the favorite of Hebrew School students because at the end of the song comes the tremendous shout: "*ZUM.*" Hebrew School walls being what they are, the shout easily disrupts not only the class doing the singing, but the entire school. The song has a mystical quality, with the repetition of "*zum gali gali gali*" sounding like a Hebrew mantra, but the reality is much less glamorous than the myth:

Tra-la-la-la, tra-la-la-la
Tra-la-la-la, tra-la-la-la
The pioneer exists to work
And the work exists for the pioneer.
Tra-la-la-la, tra-la-la-la
Tra-la-la-la, tra-la-la-la
Tra, tra, *TRA*!

And what school assembly or, for that matter, youth group campfire, *kumsitz*, or songfest hasn't included *"Heveinu Shalom Aleichem"*? Its sophisticated lyrics account for its undying popularity:

We bring you greetings
We bring you greetings
We bring you gree-eetings
We bring you greetings, greetings, greetings.

But the all-time favorite of any Hebrew School seems to have been *"Hava Nagila."* Generations grew up with this song, recently awarded a special citation as the Greatest Musical Embarrassment in Jewish history. Every catered affair which has Jewish guests must put up with this vestige of Hebrew School torture-by-accordion, usually with a massacred version of the words, which mean, simply:

Let's be happy, let's be happy, let's be happy.
And let's rejoice.
Let's have fun, let's have fun, let's have fun.
And let's rejoice.
Perk up, perk up brothers,
Perk up brothers with a happy heart
Perk up brothers with a happy heart
Perk up brothers with a happy heart
Perk up brothers with a happy heart
Perk up brotherrrrs
Perk up brotherrrrs
With a happy heart.

The only consolation is that somewhere else, an equivalent hatchet job is being done on the tarantella and the Irish jig.

LINES MY MOTHER TOLD ME
(And Responses I Never Had the *Chutzpah* to Use)

"Children! They cause you nothing but trouble, and then they leave you!"
"Parents! They're the same, except they never leave."

"Eat—children are starving in Africa."
"So get me an envelope and call Federal Express."
OR *"Oh, you cook for them, too?"*

"You should only grow up and get married and have children like you."
"I bet Grandma wished the same thing on you. How does it feel?"

"I spend all day slaving over a hot stove, and this is the thanks I get?"
"No, we planted a tree in Israel in your honor."

"What's the matter, this week you don't like my liver? You loved it last week."
"Last week it was fresh."

"You're two hours late. You'd think a person could pick up a phone and call."
"They only gave me one call, and I figured my attorney was the best bet."

"It's chilly outside. Put on a coat."
"If I put on a coat, it will be warm outside?"

"Talking to you is like talking to a wall."
"I'm sorry, did you say something?"

"How many times do I have to tell you to clean up your room?"
"By my count, at least 5,748."

"I'm not your maid."
"Gee, it was all that cooking, cleaning, and shopping that fooled me."

Summer Camp:
Adventures in Parasites

Pack your Benettons and polish your Reeboks—it's summer time and time for camp. Since the days when Amram and Yocheved packed little Moses into the basket and sent him to Camp Bullrushes, Jews have been sending their kids to overnight camp for the benefit of the kids and the sanity of the parents.

Upon arrival the kids will be met by Morty, who owns the camp and runs it during the summer when he isn't teaching driver education at Cherry Hill High School. As a teacher of driver ed, Morty

has developed, over the past thirty years, the blood pressure of an eighty-year-old man who smokes six packs a day and eats nothing but beef jerky. He comes to Lake Cowabunga every summer for a respite, to enjoy the fresh air, fellowship, and girls' head counselor. Morty has mutton-chop sideburns and a forehead that reaches clear to the back of his neck, but he loves the kids and calls them each by their first name—provided their first name is Slugger or Princess.

To maintain the Jewishness of the camp, every Friday night is set aside for nondenominational devotion and Jewish cultural experiences. Campers gather at dusk, wearing whites (or whatever is clean) at the Chapel, a bunch of benches under a spreading

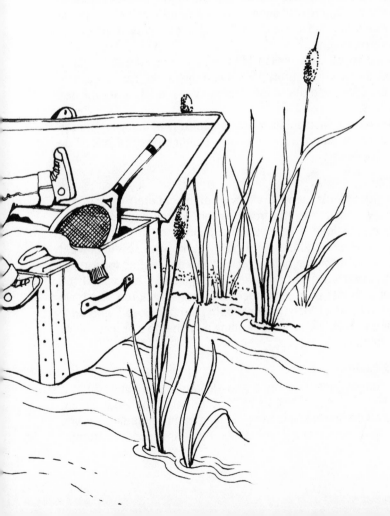

oak tree. They sing a few selections from *Fiddler on the Roof*, a couple of folk-oldies like *"Kumbaya,"* and something from Cat Stevens, who Morty insists is really named Steven Katz. One or two of the bunks have written a prayer for peace and chocolate chip cookies, and a large female counselor in small white shorts talks about the wonderful feeling of family she has at camp. All the kids in Peepers, the youngest division, start to cry out of home-sickness. At the end of the service, Morty makes everybody stand up to say *Kaddish*, the memorial prayer, for everyone who died in the Holocaust, but the kid next to you says he's going to say it for his dog. Then it's off to the dining hall for chicken soup with matzah balls which will surface at tomorrow's camper—staff baseball game. To add to the spirit of the night, challah is placed on each table, along with specimen cups filled with Welch's grape juice, which will find its way to the whitest garments in the dining hall before too long.

It used to be that Jewish kids went to one of two kinds of camps—those with Hebrew names and those with Indian names, lending credence to the theory that native Americans are the Ten Lost Tribes.

Nowadays, Jewish children are specializing at camp. There are more kinds of summer camps than a shopping mall has shoe stores. For example:

FAT CAMP
Distraught parents send their overweight children to spend a summer, exercising in the fresh air, on limited calorie intakes. Objective: to lose a few hundred pounds of unsightly flesh. Mostly these are children who have found ways to circumvent their parents' efforts at home by creatively concealing food in the laundry, videocassette boxes, and bed frames. They spend the summer with lots of other voraciously hungry children who have learned to conceal food in tennis balls, tampon boxes, and port-able radios. This is much like sending a flasher to a nudist colony for rehabilitation.

SPORTS CAMP
One no longer goes to camp to play *all* sports. One goes to play *a* sport. You can find tennis camp, soccer camp, baseball camp, basketball camp, football camp, sailing camp, horseback riding camp, table tennis camp. Hadassah has announced the forma-

tion of a canasta camp for next summer, and the Lubavitch Hassidim are starting a shuckling camp, for those who want to train to sway back and forth really fast when they pray.

COMPUTER CAMP
Here's fun. Go up to some peaceful setting by a lake, surrounded by all the miracles of creation and unbounded opportunity to commune with nature, and spend eight hours a day looking at a monochrome monitor display instructions on how to break into a TRW computer and screw up your Hebrew School principal's Visa card.

DIVORCE CAMP
Children from divorced families, or those considering divorce, go to this camp to learn to cope. To add to the reality, counselors fight with each other constantly and then leave abruptly every two weeks.

CANTORIAL CAMP
Parents who have dreams of their sons becoming cantors send them to this special music camp. For hours each day, they practice Jewish ritual music, facial contortion, bugging out their eyes, and balancing those high yarmulkes (with the pom-poms) on their heads. Each year they put on the official camp play: *The Jazz Singer*.

DOCTOR CAMP
Aspiring physicians spend the summer dissecting woodland creatures and investing in real estate.

ATTORNEY CAMP
Lawyers-to-be enjoy the pleasures of preparing malpractice cases on behalf of the woodland creatures who wander into Doctor Camp.

HEALTH CLUB CAMP
Belonging to a health club is not the same as using a health club, and that's why this camp exists. There are coordination drills—coordination of workout apparel, coordination of lunch hour and racquetball leagues, coordination of strained muscles and impending aerobics classes. Campers become fluent in clubspeak,

using words like graphite and Nautilus frequently, and discussing the relative merits of the Stairmaster and the treadmill without ever having been on either. Counselors are former health club employees with names like Darcy and Helmut, and have bodies which make normal people say, "Oh, what's the use?"

Some things about camps have not changed in the least. For one, they inspire unswerving loyalty on the part of the campers. Never

mind that little Ashley spent four weeks sleeping in things she used to step around before wilderness survival camp—she will cry to the point of hyperventilation on the day Camp Rambo ends. Long after his Haftarah is a distant memory, the words to "Dry Sheets, My Camp Dry Sheets" will float through Jamie's reveries. Before too long, a second generation of campers will be packed off by their nostalgic parents to enjoy the Indian lore at Camp No-Thum-Suk.

The Bar/Bat Mitzvah

Just at the time when a boy's face begins to bloom with the topographic features of Colorado and his voice sounds so much like his mother's that people on the telephone call him ma'am; just at a time when a girl looks in the mirror and sees that wisp of dark hair on her upper lip and realizes that there is something indescribably humorous about baby fat and training bras; tradition insists that they stand in front of just about everybody they've ever known, with God and the Rabbi looking over a shoulder, and demonstrate how lucky they are to become an adult. Yes, it is that wonderful time called Bar Mitzvah (for a boy) and Bat Mitzvah* (for a girl).

It starts with a tape recording. Many fathers have made fools of themselves, bursting into their daughters' rooms enraged, looking for the guy whose voice is filtering down the steps at ten o'clock at night, only to find out it is the Cantor, chanting a part of the Book of Prophets called the Haftarah. The tape plays continually, as if on a loop. Parents find themselves whistling the chant in the shower. Five-year-old brother Jeremy sings it between "Row, Row, Row Your Boat" and "Yankee Doodle." Even the maid knows the words and the tune. Only the thirteen-year-old seems unable to learn the lilting chant of this section of the Holy Scriptures.

Actually, the service is the easy part. It is mostly the memorization of age-old prayers and chants, reading of speeches doctored—or even written—by the Rabbi ("Dear God: As I stand before Thy holy Torah today, prepared to assume the responsibili-

*Sometimes pronounced Bas Mitzvah by those who haven't been to one in fifteen years.

ties of a pious and devoted Jew[ess] . . .), and sitting still for somewhere between an hour and three. What's really tough is the reception.

Advice to Parents

The first thing to do is to decide on a budget. Begin by saying, "This affair need not be ostentatious and expensive," and decide on a figure that is both generous and sensible. Then show it to the caterer. He will say, "Oh, this affair is for immediate family only? It is proper to invite the grandparents, you know."

Next, you'll need a band. You will want a professional group, able to appeal to the three generations which will be represented. Don't fight the inevitable—you will wind up hiring a group called Harry Horowitz and His Hawaiians or Morris Mendelson's Music Machine.

The kid will want a DJ. Don't give in. You must have *some* standard for the types of people with whom you will associate. Give the band a list of songs they must play. No matter what you include, tradition and union contracts require that eight songs be played during the course of the affair. Though the list occasionally changes, the current selections include:

> "Sunrise, Sunset"
>
> "*Hava Nagila*"
>
> "More"
>
> "Girl from Ipanema"
>
> "Feelings"
>
> "*Siman Tov u'Mazal Tov*" (bumped the Bunny Hop during the Jewish renaissance following the Six-Day War)
>
> "You Light Up My Life"
>
> "Celebrate Good Times"

Invitation lists are difficult, but if you divide the potential guests into two groups, it will go much more smoothly. First are the must-invites. They include:

> • Immediate relatives
> • Anyone crucial to your business
> • Any cousin who has invited you to a similar function
> • All of the children in your child's Hebrew School class

- Anyone you carpool with
- The grandmother's bridge club
- The grandfather's poker buddies
- That couple you met on the cruise last year
- Your housekeeper
- The Rabbi
- The Cantor
- The Hebrew School principal and teachers
- At least one Black person so that everyone can turn around and look when he or she walks in

The second group is made up of alternates. These are people who get invitations as the must-invites decline their invitations. They include:

- People you *want* to invite because you like them
- The child's friends

As the invitation responses pour in, be sure to make a list of friends and relatives who are in from out of town. Instruct the bandleader to read these names just before dessert is served. He must say, "Who came all the way from" before each city, even if it is the next town over.

Seating arrangements are comparatively easy. *Goyim* sit with *goyim*. The Rabbi and other members of the synagogue staff sit together, even if they can't stand each other. You may also put cousin Irving, who spent a year on a religious kibbutz, at this table, because he and the Rabbi will have so much to talk about. Your sister's ex-husband, who always sends a nice gift, may sit with anyone except those related to your sister. Best bet—seat him with the *goyim*. Anyone whose RSVP arrived late gets to sit with the children, preferably with uninvited children whose parents don't know that an invitation addressed to "Mr. and Mrs." does not mean "and their four children."

At the head table, in the center, sits the child of the hour, flanked by parents and then respective grandparents.

Proper Dress Is Essential
Outfitting the entire family is important. It goes without saying that parents and brothers and sisters get new clothes for the oc-

casion. Special care must be given in selecting the Mitzvah suit or dress for the child. Be prepared to spend between two and three thousand dollars.

For starters, this is not the time to shop at J.C. Penney's. Your child is going to read from the Torah, which is written on lambskin parchment, not polyester—and not just any lambskin parchment, mind you.

The kid gets a first pair of real leather shoes. Gucci is preferable. A girl gets heels, unless the Rabbi is short, in which case flats are an absolute necessity. A boy gets dress socks, which he will never wear again, and which will drop around his ankles as he begins the ceremony. Everyone wears brand-new underwear, just in case. . . .

A boy gets a suit, three pieces, preferably pinstriped. It isn't necessary to get something custom made, but people should see at least Bill Blass's name when the kid puts those envelopes in his inside jacket pocket. And buy him a real tie. Clip-on ties are not only gauche, but they tend to pop off when the boy hits the high notes in his Haftarah. Don't rent him a tux for the reception—he'll look like a maitre d'.

A girl gets a white frilly dress, long-sleeved in an Orthodox synagogue, mid-sleeved in a Conservative congregation, and strapless in a Reform temple. Since most girls have grown to their Prom Night height by age thirteen, it's probably worth the investment in a Kamali-look, she'll get more use out of it than the wedding dress, and that one will cost six grand.

So far, you have spent about $450, tops. Add to this figure a maximum of $80 for a really good haircut or beauty salon treatment and you are left with funds for the last piece of necessary apparel.

Six weeks before the event, your orthodontist will inform you that unless your child is fitted with a full set of braces in the next thirty days, he or she will develop a permanent overbite that will enable him or her to eat the far side of an ear of corn. There is an advantage to this development, thanks to modern technology. With proper tuning, the braces can pick up FM broadcasts, allowing you to transmit the now-familiar tape directly to the microphone on the pulpit, which will make your child sound exactly like the Cantor simply by lip-synching.

The Reception

At the reception, every member of the family is expected to make a toast. Recommended texts are as follows:

Mother:
> "I always dreamed of this day, from the time I changed your dirty diapers in the middle of the night to the time you ran naked out the front door to avoid taking a bath to the time we caught you necking with the Goldberg boy/girl from next door...."

Father:
> "Well, now that you've finished all of your Jewish education you can go back to mowing the lawn on Saturday morning instead of having to go to Temple all the time...."

Brother:
> "I guess you aren't so bad, except when you won't let me hang around with your friends. Mom says I should say I love you and give you a kiss, but you can forget that part...."

Sister:
> "Being your little sister is one of the greatest challenges a woman can face in the world today...."

Bar Mitzvah:
> "Thank you all for the great gifts you gave me, especially those of you considerate enough to let me know where I can return them...."

Bat Mitzvah:
> "I chose the theme of 'unicorns' for my party because they remind me of my boyfriend...."

Perhaps the most important preparation for the celebration is to sew big pockets into the Bar Mitzvah suit, or give the Bat Mitzvah a large pocketbook. By the end of the evening, they will be filled with envelopes from friends and relatives who either forgot to buy a present or aren't creative enough to come up with a gift idea. Parents: Confiscate all of the envelopes. Give your child $50 to spend as he or she pleases, and then tell the kid the rest went into a "college fund." With any luck, you can pay off the caterer with the proceeds from the party.

Teach Your Children Well:
A Guide to the Human Body

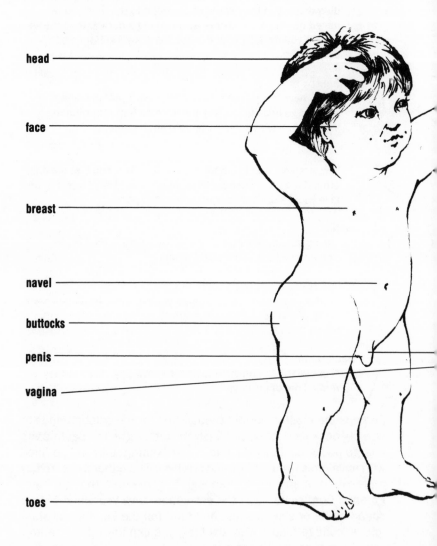

head ——————————————

face ——————————————

breast ——————————————

navel ——————————————

buttocks ——————————————

penis ——————————————

vagina ——————————————

toes ——————————————

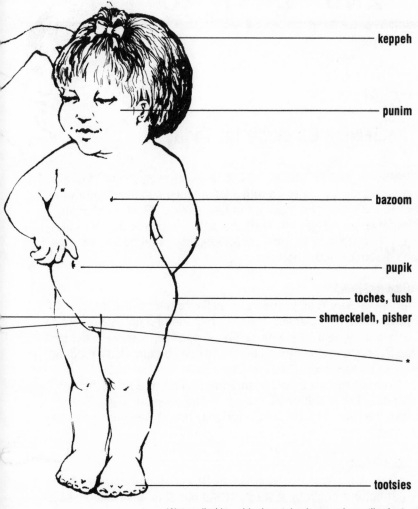

keppeh

punim

bazoom

pupik

toches, tush

shmeckeleh, pisher

*

tootsies

*Not applicable—girls do not develop a vagina until puberty.

EXODUS

PASSOVER, OTHER HOLIDAYS, AND WHAT TO EAT

The Jewish Calendar for Today

Traditional Jewish holidays are often a mystery, even to Jews, whose minds are cluttered with a lot of folk wisdom and family innovations ("Children must go to bed early on Rosh Hashanah," "Daddies are allowed to read the paper in peace on Shavuot," etc.). Here then is a comprehensive guide to the real meanings and practices of the holidays:

ROSH HASHANAH

The Jewish New Year is celebrated in September to avoid the last-minute rush in December. The theme of the first of the High Holy Days is Judgment. God sits before an open book as we pass by, one by one, and if we're very quiet and don't disturb God's reading we can usually avoid the Final Decree.

To remind us to repent, a ram's horn is blown. Getting the right sounds out of it is difficult, though it is much easier if you first remove the ram. Reform Jews often play Benny Goodman records instead.

YOM KIPPUR

Ten days after Rosh Hashanah is the Day of Atonement, on which we afflict our souls by fasting, listing our sins, and listening to the president of the synagogue ask for pledges. On this day, each person's destiny is sealed, with God decreeing, as it says in the prayerbook: "Who shall live and who shall die: who shall perish by sword, who by earthquake, who by fire, who by disease, and who by bad advice on the Stock Options market."

SUKKOT

The Feast of Booths recalls how the Israelites wandered in the desert for forty years in temporary housing. They blamed Moses for the long delay, but Moses insisted it was the contractor's fault. In

memory of this, for seven days we live in huts made of organic material and natural fibers, decorating them with fruits and vegetables which, as we know, grow in wild abundance in the desert.

CHANUKKAH

Originally, Chanukkah was a single-night celebration. It commemorated how a small band of guerrillas, the Maccabees, defeated an evil Assyrian regime by getting them involved in an unpopular land war in Asia, causing dissent and student uprisings at home. When Christmas was invented, with all its gift-giving and decorations, the Jews upped the ante by extending Chanukkah to eight days and lighting candles. Christmas was then extended to twelve days, and the Jews folded, unable to beat twelve drummers drumming, five golden rings, and a partridge in a pear tree.

PURIM

Purim means "lots," which gives rise to the question "lots of what?" Long before Halloween, Jews dressed up in costume to celebrate Purim. Why? Because it is lots of fun—that's why the holiday is called Purim. The story behind the holiday is that Queen Esther of Persia, a Jew, saved her people from destruction at the hands of the evil vizier, Haman, by getting her husband, King Ahashverosh, drunk on lots of wine. That's why the holiday is called Purim. Esther's uncle Mordecai was named to take Haman's place. From his high post, Mordecai bought up all the available real estate, particularly undeveloped lots, which is why the holiday is called Purim.

PESACH

Also known as Passover, this holiday celebrates the exodus of the Jews from Egypt. The holiday begins in the middle of the Hebrew month Nissan, which is the time of the year new Japanese cars appear on the market. Jews avoid anything with leavening and eat, instead, a flat cracker called matzah, which can be eaten plain, toasted, or fried without losing the distinctive taste of cardboard. This is to remind us that while Pharoah was out supervising the pyramids, rebellious Jews were building his palace out of substandard materials.

Today Jews celebrate by having a huge feast called a Seder, marked by the retelling of the story of the exodus. It was traditional in the past to dine on couches, necessitating four cups of wine to wash them down. What with the cost of furniture these days, most people serve brisket or turkey instead.

SHAVUOT

The trendiest ancient holiday is Shavuot, the Feast of Weeks. This harvest festival commemorates the giving of the Ten Commandments, but has a different appeal today. While the other holidays drag on for seven or eight or nine days, Shavuot is short—just a day or two. In today's busy world, it is seen as quality time with God.

TISHA B'AV

On the hottest day of the summer, Jews recall the destruction of the Temple, the razing of Jerusalem, purges, pogroms, exiles, expulsions, massacres, and inquisitions by fasting, weeping and wailing, and unplugging the air conditioner. Never let it be said we don't know how to have a good time.

However, new dates have found their way onto the calendar in America, including:

May 7—YOM HÄAGEN-DAZS
This observance commemorates the introduction of the first premium ice cream, invented by a Jew, to supermarket shelves. Incidentally, the name Häagen-Dazs is really Hebrew for "Cholesterol-Overdose."

June 22—CAMP BEGINS
The day on which ninety-four percent of all Jewish children between the ages of nine and fifteen go off to summer camp is observed by Jewish adults in Chinese restaurants all over the country.

September 21—CUBS CLINCH NATIONAL LEAGUE EAST CHAMPIONSHIPS
The Chicago Cubs are baseball's answer to the Jews. Waiting for redemption after more than forty years wandering in the wilderness of afternoon baseball, on this day in 1984 the Cubs finally made it to the top. Could the Messiah be far behind?

September 28—CUBS BLOW NATIONAL LEAGUE PENNANT
Oh well. As the old saying goes: Wait till next year in Jerusalem.

January 28th—HUBERT HUMPHREY'S *YAHRTZEIT*
The anniversary of Hubert Humphrey's death marks the official end of the traditional involvement of Jews in liberal Democratic Party politics.

March 16—BOB DYLAN'S RETURN TO JUDAISM
Not since Spinoza have Jews held their collective breath with such trepidation as when "Slow Train Comin'" hit the record stores. After a period of uncertainty, it was on this day that word of Dylan's appearance in a synagogue was leaked to *Variety*.

The Yuppie Haggadah

The traditional Haggadah is hopelessly out of date. For example, how can you pray fervently "Next Year in Jerusalem" when you already went there in high school and where you really hope to be next spring is Club Med in the Bahamas?

To add life to tired Haggadic bones, herewith are excerpts from a brand new Haggadah, soon to be released by the J.D.L. Press under its *Publish or Perish!* imprint.

FOUR QUESTIONS
(The youngest chants the following):

> *1) Why is this night different from all other nights (first night add: except, of course, for tomorrow night)?*
>
> *2) On all other nights we eat bread, croissants, even bran muffins; why on this night do we eat matzah?*
>
> *3) On all other nights we sit straight or get noodged about our posture, unless eating sushi in a Japanese restaurant; why on this night do we eat reclining?*
>
> *4) On all other nights we do not dip once, unless eating fondue; why on this night do we dip twice?*

MA-ASEH

It is related of Rabbi Ben Zoma, Rabbi Ben Epstein, Rabbi Tarphon, and Rabbi Jose the Galilean, that they once spent Passover eve at the Holiday Inn in Bene Berak. And they retold the story of the Exodus from Egypt until Rabbi Tarphon said, "I am now seventy years old and never before met a rabbi with a Mexican name like Jose."

Whereupon Rabbi Jose said, "With a name like Tarphon, I wouldn't joke." And he continued, "The Bible says we must remember the Exodus all the days of our lives. The 'days of our lives' means just days. 'All the days of our lives' includes evenings and weekends."

Ben Zoma, on the other hand, expounded, "'The Days of Our Lives' *means* The Days of Our Lives *only. 'All the* Days of Our Lives' *includes* Search for Tomorrow.*" And they argued thusly until their pupils came and told them, "Our Masters! The time has come for your morning aerobics!"*

FOUR SONS

The Torah speaks of four sons: the wise (Groucho), the wicked (Chico), the one nobody likes (Zeppo), and the one unable to ask (Harpo). The wise son,

what does he say? *"I shot an elephant in my pajamas. How did it get in my pajamas?"* To him reply:

> Rabbi Simeon ben Gamliel said, *"The world is based on three principles: truth, justice, and peace."* Simeon the Just said, *"The three principles are learning, worship, and kindness. Gamliel, what did he know?"* Joshua ben Perachya said, *"Get yourself a teacher; ac-*

quire a companion, perhaps a Lhasa apso; invest not in computers; buy a condo."

If he cries out, "That's no answer!" respond, "Don't get wise with me."

The one unable to speak, what do you say to him? "Praise the Lord with lute and timbrel, with flute and jazz piano, with bulbhorn and harp, with shuckling and kibbitzing."

The wicked son, what does he say? "What do you mean by this service?" By saying "you" instead of "we" he shuts himself off from the people of Israel. Strike him on the head with a shmurah matzah and ignore the question. If he persists, threaten him with a writ of Habeas Karpas.

THREE SYMBOLS

Rabban Gamliel used to say that if you failed to explain three symbols, it is as if you stepped on a crack and broke your mother's back. These are:

THE PAYSOP: a payroll-based employee stock ownership plan created by the Pharoahs. Because the Israelites found notice of their eligibility to participate posted on their doorposts, many remained behind in Egypt to become shareholders in Ramses's contraceptive business.

THE MAZDA: unleavened Cadillac which the Israelites drove from Egypt because their mechanics failed to rise. It inspired the Psalmist: "Salvation, yea, and foreign cars come from the Lord; but whence parts and labor?"

THE MORTAR: a mixture of brick chips and duco cement placed on the seder plate to remind us that our ancestors in Egypt were forced to eat a mortarlike mixture of apples, nuts, and wine.

"CHAD GADYA"

Then came the Angel of Death, who killed the butcher who slaughtered the ox who worried the cat that killed the rat that ate the malt that lived in the house that Jack built.

CONCLUSION

O Lord, we have observed the Passover seder in accordance with all statutes and ordinances, albeit interpreted conveniently to minimize inconvenience. We hope you will be satisfied and forgive us the croutons. Unite us, your people of Israel, where we can be in the majority for a change, as it is written: "I want to be a part of it, New York, New York."

David Wolper Presents the 3,000th Anniversary of the Ten Commandments

Basking in the glow of his success with the Olympics and Liberty Weekend, producer David Wolper has announced his next assignment: the 3,000th anniversary of the Ten Commandments. Although it is suspected that the 3,000th anniversary was over 250 years ago, Wolper has planned a retrospective celebration to commemorate the role the Big Ten has played in our lives.

Festivities begin in Cairo on the first night of Passover. Host Charlton Heston will lead a group of 50,000 Jews named Levi (sponsored by the company of the same name) in the slaughter of 50,000 lambs, which will then be roasted and air-shipped to the hungry and homeless in the States and in Africa. In the USA, the project is being called "Lambs Across America." Elsewhere, the effort is known as "Ewe S. Aid for Africa." To begin the reenactment of the Exodus, President Hosni Mubarak of Egypt will ceremonially throw out the first Jew.

At midnight, the largest marching band assembled in history, 600,000 students from Hebrew Schools all over the world, will march out of Egypt and into the Sinai Desert. Selections will include "Let My People Go," "Ahab the A-rab," "Don't Think Twice, It's All Right," and a special appearance by Lionel Ritchie singing "All Night Long."

Wolper plans to work with the Universal Studios Tour to recreate the parting of the Red Sea at the actual site of the parting of the Red Sea. Patrons paying $5,000 apiece will be seated on the deck of the aircraft carrier *Nimitz* to witness the technological miracle.

But the biggest extravaganza will occur at the foot of Mount Sinai. For the occasion, the entire Sinai Desert will be transformed into a giant amphitheater. Leaders of various religions will be invited to deliver a five-minute talk entitled "What the Ten Commandments Mean to Me." To this point, commitments have been received from the Pope, the Ayatollah Khomeini, Sun Myung Moon, and Werner Erhardt.

Following the serious part of the program, a halftime show featuring Great Tens of World History will be presented. Included will be Ten Little Indians, the Top Ten Songs of Rock 'n' Roll History, the Ten O'Clock News, the Big Ten College Sports Conference, and Bo Derek.

As darkness settles, Heston will ascend Mount Sinai. When he reaches the top, to recreate the "thunders and lightning and voice of the horn waxing and waning," the largest fireworks extravaganza in the history of the universe will be displayed from the mountain peak. The band will play "You Light Up My Life."

The conclusion of the fireworks will feature a giant "10" created by lasers and explosives, after which the dust will settle and Heston will appear carrying the two tablets of the law. At this point, the audience will be asked to affix the special lenses to their flashlights, provided by Eveready, and at the count of three, turn them on. A giant golden calf will be formed by the assembled throng. Heston will cast the tablets down to a prearranged spot, where they will explode in a cloud of smoke.

When the smoke clears, the grand finale begins. Standing on a platform at the top of the mountain, George Burns will read "The New Ten Commandments," specially revised for the 21st century:

> 1. I am the Lord your God who brought you out of the Egyptian house of bondage and delivered you to the International House of Pancakes.

> 2. You shall make no graven image of Me, unless you make Me look like Tom Selleck or Catherine Deneuve.

> 3. My last name is not "Dammit," dammit.

> 4. Remember the Sabbath day?

> 5. Honor your father and your mother with a testimonial at the Waldorf on their fiftieth anniversary and a phone call on their birthdays.

> 6. You shall not murder unless you are approached on the subway by three hoodlums asking for change for video games.

7. You shall not commit adultery, especially in the State of Georgia.

8. You shall not steal unless elected to public office.

9. You shall not witness false bears.

10. You shall not covert. So get out of Nicaragua.

Burns will then turn the program over to Kool and the Gang for the farewell number, "Celebrate Good Times," after which buses will take the audience into the Promised Land.

The Fine Art of
What to Serve for Every Occasion

Face it—we are insecure without food. Maybe it is the result of a history of poverty and deprivation. Maybe the heritage of dietary restrictions gives us a certain passion for that which is permitted. Maybe we heard "Eat—children are starving in Europe" so often that we subconsciously feel we are doing our part for world hunger by putting out a little *nosh*. So, unlike in some cultures, the question is never *should* you put out a little something to eat, but *what* should that little something be.

Take the traditional Sabbath meal. Every generation has its own way of observing Friday night's dinner ritual, creating new traditions out of old (see next page).

The question of quantity looms over food preparation. God forbid there shouldn't be enough! Therefore, always assume that everyone who is coming will want to eat a large serving of everything you put out. So, if you are having three couples over for dessert, make eight servings of cheesecake, eight servings of spongecake, and eight servings of chocolate layer cake. And a large fruit salad in case someone is on a diet. Don't worry—you can freeze the leftovers.

Never eat your own food. Always use the excuse, "I want to be sure there's enough." However, it is permissible to have "just a taste" of whatever is on the plate of your spouse, children, or best friends.

Become acquainted with the feeding habits of our forest friends. At various times you will be called upon to compare the eating habits of your guests and the animal kingdom. Be sure you know the difference between "He eats like a bird" and "He eats like a pig." One refers to quantity, the other to manners.

Buy those cute little recipe cards and fill them out with whatever you are serving, because any polite guest will ask you for the recipe of your offerings. No recipe is too simple for a card, because anyone who asks for the recipe for the scrambled eggs you served at brunch needs to be told that you "crack the eggs into a bowl and throw away the shells."

CHALLAH MIT CHOPPED LIVER

MATZOH BALL SOUP

BOILED CHICKEN

TZIMMES

KASHA

GREEN BEANS

MANDEL BROT

SANKA OR SWEE-TOUCH-NEE

US

GRANDMA & GRANDPA

pâté de foie gras · baguette
consommé
poulet au pôt
honey glazed carrots · fruit garni
rice pilaf
haricots verts
almond torte
decaffeinated espresso

41

CHICKEN, THE WONDER FOOD

The ancient Egyptians had the Divine Lamb, the Indians have the Sacred Cow, Amos and Andy had the Holy Mackerel. Jews have the Magic Chicken. Though the Holy Temple was destroyed centuries ago, Jews remember the ancient sacrifices thanks to the Fantastic Fowl which is boiled, broiled, braised, baked, barbequed, and, not infrequently, burned. Never is its mystical power so great, however, than when it is simmered with roots and herbs to make the Sacred Soup.

Chicken soup can cure anything. Got a cold? A little chicken soup will clear those sinuses right away. Depressed? Chicken soup will cheer you up. Nuclear test ban treaty negotiations stalled? A bit of the broth will pave the way to world peace.

Every grandmother has a secret recipe for The Soup. Ingredients, however, are less important than preparation:

> THURSDAY MORNING: Fill the biggest pot in the house ¾ full with cold water. Add one chicken, cut up in eighths. (Necks, feet, and gizzards are nice touches.) Put in the rest of the ingredients. Turn up the heat to the highest setting; cover pot. When water begins to boil, stir once, put lid back on, and turn heat to simmer.
>
> FRIDAY, 2:56 AM: Wake up with a start, and say, "Oh my God, I forgot to turn off the soup!" Turn off the soup.
>
> FRIDAY, 3:08 PM: Skim off the fat. Add salt and pepper to taste.*

Serve too hot to eat, with ice cube garnish.

*Some add this step: Ask spouse to taste. Add water because she/he says it is too salty. Wait till spouse leaves room. Add salt. This may continue all day, potentially doubling yield of recipe.

Kosher, Kosher Style, Biblical Kosher, and the Reuben Sandwich

Does anyone really understand the Jewish dietary laws? Oh, some people will tell you they do, but they are just betting that you know even less than they do. In fact, one reason Jews have always emphasized education is that you need an advanced degree just to understand what you can and cannot eat.

Biblical guidelines are pretty straightforward. No pork, no shrimp, no lobster. The original reasons for these prohibitions are

lost in history, but it is a sure bet that Moses never ate Chinese or things might have been a lot different.

Everyone who keeps kosher will tell you that his version is the only correct version. Everyone else is either a fanatic or a heretic. Modern scholars are convinced that God created fruits and vegetables so that Orthodox Jews wouldn't starve to death if trapped inside a Reform temple for any period of time.

True kosher requires the supervision of a Rabbi. What, then, is "kosher style"? Kosher style is to kosher what textured vinyl is to leather—a completely inadequate imitation. Mr. Vlasic can no sooner lay claim to the kosher pickle than Mr. Manischewitz can turn out an authentic kielbasa. Nonetheless, kosher style restaurants continue to churn out that aberration known as the Reuben Sandwich.

Since it mixes dairy and meat products, strictly forbidden by the dietary laws, it can hardly be considered kosher. Actually, the sandwich was named on the Lower East Side of New York City in 1923. Reuben Goldfarb, an anarchist from Moscow, was standing on the corner of Grand and Essex denouncing the stranglehold the local rabbis had on the restaurant trade. He held in his left hand a quarter pound of corned beef, and in his right a slice of swiss cheese. Just as he was reaching a fevered pitch about how they couldn't be found in the same store in all of the neighborhood, a bread delivery wagon went out of control and fell on the unsuspecting soap-box orator, crushing him to death. Ever since that time, corned beef and swiss on rye with Russian dressing has been known as the Reuben.

Some people claim to observe "biblical kosher." They mean they just don't eat pork or boil a kid in its mother's milk. It pays to be suspicious of people so dedicated to such biblical practices. In fact, if you see them smearing the blood of a lamb on their door-posts, you might want to send your firstborn to Toledo for the weekend.

"What Am I, Chopped Liver?"

The famous sarcastic remark used by Jews to call attention to their own qualifications has a long and proud history in our tradition. Tracing the origins of this phrase has given us insights into the psycholinguistic development of our people.

The earliest reference to this phrase is from recently discovered fragments of the Book of Exodus, alluding to a section not found in the biblical canon. As best as scholars can reconstruct it, the segment occurs on Moses's first visit to Pharoah:

> . . . whereupon Moses spake to Pharoah, saying, "Let my people go!" Saith Pharoah, "And by what power dost thou claimeth my slaves?" And Moses said, "By the power of their One True Master." And Pharoah said, "What beist I, roasted lamb?"

Pharoah's comment proved oddly prophetic. In later history, the first woman leader of Israel, Deborah, sat beneath the tree where she dispensed her judgments. Barak, captain of the army, came to see her, complaining that there was no one to deliver the prebattle peptalk to the troops. Deborah is reported to have responded, "What am I, camel dung?"

In Talmudic times, the most famous of the sages was Rabbi Hil-

lel, who first used the contemporary phrase in his maxim on Looking Out for Number One:

> If I am not for myself, then who will be for me?
> And if I am for myself alone, then what am I, chopped liver?

Slight variations have been found among Jews in different cultures. A Jew arrested for stealing in Moslem Spain was said to have remarked to the judge at his sentencing, "What am I, chopped fingers?" During the French Revolution, François Jean-Pierre Katz, close advisor to King Louis XVI, spoke these words as he was led to the guillotine, "*Zut alors! Je suis le pâté de foie gras!*"

Revisionists wrongly attribute the origin of the phrase to more contemporary times. The current theory suggests that the exclamation was coined by an incompetent waiter at the Second Avenue Deli in New York, who, having mixed up his order for the umpteenth time, proclaimed, "What am I, chopped liver?" But as you can see, the phrase is much more deeply rooted.

Contemporary variations are many. In areas where Jewish and Chinese neighborhoods adjoin, it is not unusual to hear, "What am I, chop suey?" In California, land of raised consciousness, animal-rights activists have begun to substitute, "What am I, mashed tofu?"—but only vegetarians find this a satisfying substitute.

LEVITICUS

RELIGION AND RABBIS
(AND OTHER JEWS)

The Real Difference Between Reform, Conservative, and Orthodox—and Others

There are so many versions of Judaism, sometimes it's hard to know which one is the authentic one. This handy guide will clear up all confusion:

ORTHODOXY
Orthodox Jews believe that God revealed the Torah to Moses, as well as the Talmud, the dietary laws, who to vote for in 1996, and the winning lottery numbers in Massachusetts Megabucks. For them, there is no such thing as change in the law, so they round off to the nearest dollar. Women enjoy an exalted position in Orthodox synagogues—usually the second balcony. Because Orthodoxy represents an unbroken chain with Judaism's forebearers, it alone is authentic.

CONSERVATIVE
Most Conservative Jews are liberals, and this confusion of identities has spilled into Conservative Judaism. In fact, the Conservative movement has no luck when it comes to communicating what it believes. In Israel, they took the Hebrew name *Mesorati*, which means "traditional," but everyone thinks they sell Italian sportscars. Conservative rabbis believe that they are the heirs to the

sages of the Talmud, and follow that tradition by publicly disagreeing whenever possible. Because Conservatism represents an unbroken chain with Judaism's forebearers, it alone is authentic.

REFORM
Reform Jews believe in education, and send all their children to Reform Schools. There they learn to appreciate the message of the mentors of the movement, Isaac Mayer Wise and Stephen S. Wise, known in the inner circle as the Wise Guys. Reform Jews believe that everyone has to decide for himself or herself what is important in Judaism, except for synagogue dues, which are decided for you. Because Reform represents an unbroken chain with Judaism's forebearers, it alone is authentic.

RECONSTRUCTIONISM
Nobody really knows what Reconstructionism is except Mordecai Kaplan who invented it, and he died.Reconstructionist Jews don't believe in a supernatural God. Instead, they believe God wears a three-piece suit and commutes to the city every day from Long Island, just like the rest of us. There, He holds a number of city contracts for renovating historical landmarks, hence the name Reconstructionist Judaism. This is why Reconstructionist Jews, who don't really believe in prayer, can nonetheless pray for the rebuilding of the Temple, which they don't really want rebuilt. They just have a bid in on the project. Because Reconstructionism represents an unbroken chain with Judaism's forebearers, it alone is authentic.

New movements in Judaism are springing up all the time. Fast-trackers in this generation include:

ORTHODONTISM
This group believes that if tradition is to be preserved, enforcement of the Law must have some teeth, and those teeth might as well be straight.

CONFORM
This is a blend of Conservative and Reform, whose motto is "Let's see what everyone else is doing before we decide."

RESERVATIVE
Another offshoot of Reform and Conservative, these Jews emphasize not only a belief in the afterlife, but the importance of calling ahead to assure yourself a place.

PENTATHODOXY
A new branch of Orthodoxy which emphasizes not just academic proficiency, but the ability to swim, run, bike, cross-country ski, and slay giants with a slingshot in the fastest possible time. Very popular in urban areas. Lapsed members who return often join the Refirm movement instead.

RECONSIDERISM
An important part of Judaism is gathering—for worship, for study, for fellowship. This group gathers to make public pronouncements on political issues and then to clarify or reverse their original positions.

Believing in God

Do Jews believe in God? Yes, we do. We believed in God when everyone else was praying to rocks and trees.What we don't have is that formal relationship which typifies religions which haven't known God so long. Our relationship with God is relaxed and comfortable, like an old friend you haven't seen for a long time, but with whom you can pick up wherever you left off whenever you get together.

Our problem is that God's name keeps changing on us. Our sages assured us that every generation has its own relationship with God, but that does cause a certain amount of confusion. Here's a sampling of God's *a.k.a.*'s:

SHIELD OF ABRAHAM
The first Jew, Abraham, was always getting into trouble with local potentates who accused him of being clannish, taking up all the spaces in medical schools, and trying to dominate the international banking system. He needed a lot of help.

FEAR OF ISAAC
If God had commanded your father to tie you up and sacrifice you, you'd be a little skittish, too.

STRENGTH OF JACOB
Anyone with thirteen children had to get that day-to-day stamina from somewhere.

ROCK OF ISRAEL
Often, this name is used in contrast to hell, sometimes known as "the hard place"—hence the expression.

MASTER OF THE UNIVERSE
Not to be confused with He-Man and She-Ra.

I-WILL-BE-WHAT-I-WILL-BE
God gave this name to Moses at the burning bush, adding, "But you can just call me I-will-be."

LORD OF HOSTS
This name was first revealed to TV personality Monty Hall.

Perhaps this continuously growing list has been the impediment to the prophetic vision of a day on which "God's name will be one."

HEAVEN AND HELL

The most misunderstood aspect of Judaism is the matter of life after death. Non-Jews are nonplussed to discover that the ideas of heaven and hell really don't exist in our tradition. Sure, there are all kinds of stories about heavenly rewards and all sorts of longings for a perfect World-to-Come, but Jews don't really believe in Dante's *Inferno* or in James Mason putting Warren Beatty on an SST to his eternal reward.

So where do Jews go when they die?

Miami.

Rear View of Heads Are a Key to Denomination

Conservative

Hassid

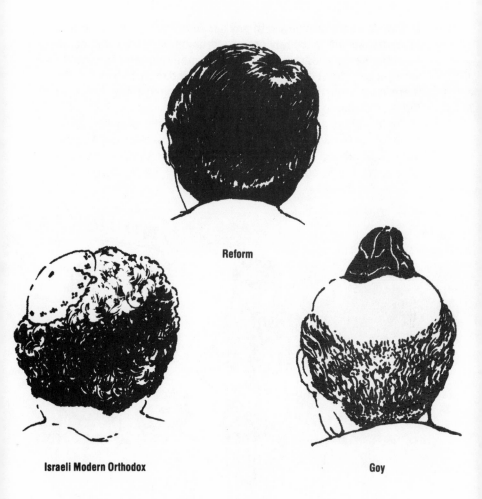

Reform

Israeli Modern Orthodox

Goy

53

Minsk, Bialystock, and Slobodtka, Attorneys-at-Law

In Grandpa's day any Jew with any sense of history belonged to a *landsmanschaft*, a loosely organized union of people who came from the same geographic area in Europe. Mom and Dad fell in with the gang from the old neighborhood, and remained close with them long after the old neighborhood changed from Jewish to Black to Hispanic to Asian.

Today, things are different. We feel a little silly organizing The Order of Tom's River or The Fraternal Lodge of Skokie-ites, and the old neighborhood consisted of a series of tract homes half-an-acre apart, hardly conducive to intimacy. Still, we must find ways

Shtupple   Yuts   Shlepper

to categorize and organize ourselves. The modern Jew falls into one of these categories:

SUBURBAN HIGH-TECH UPWARDLY MOBILE (SHTUPPIE)
Check out the den in this family's split-level and you will think you are in the Sharper Image showroom. Jewish objects include an electric Chanukkah lamp on an eight-day timer and the entire PBS "Heritage" series on videotape. Unwatched.

YOUNG URBAN TRADITIONALISTS (YUTS)
Sometimes married, sometimes single, these people remember the good times they had in synagogue youth groups and try to recapture that spirit by getting together on Saturday morning in the library or chapel of an urban synagogue. To make the service more contemporary, they take the two-and-a-half-hour service and extend it to four hours. Babysitting provided.

Feygles   Chozir   Greps

SELF-HELPED, LAID-BACK ETHICAL PERSON (SHLEPPER)

This person has done est, primal scream, scientology, and a weekend with the Lubavitch Hassidim. He protests apartheid, nuclear proliferation, world hunger, and, something near and dear to the heart of every Jew—the treatment of whales. Impossible to argue with this person as he is constantly checking his senses: "I hear you, I see where you are coming from, I feel your vibes," etc. He can quote to you from the Bible, by Leo Buscaglia.

FINALLY EMERGED YOUNG GAYS AND LESBIANS (FEYGLES)

Jews have always been on the cutting edge of social change, and now they are trendsetters in the alternative lifestyles of the late 20th century. Their parents are learning to apply old standards to new living arrangements, admonishing their gay sons, "It's all right to live with that *goy* for a while, but when you settle down, it should be with a nice Jewish boy."

CAMPAIGNING TO HELP ON ZIONISM AND ISRAELI RELATIONS (CHOZIR)

Twenty years ago, these young, successful business people toured Israel in dirty jeans and a sleeping bag. Last year, they took a trip with the United Jewish Appeal, stayed in a five-star hotel, and ate kosher Chinese food. Now, they are constantly on the phone asking you either to contribute to the cause or write your congressman to stop the sale of PVC pipe to Kuwait ("You never know what those terrorists might do with it").

GASTRONOMICALLY REAWAKENED ETHNIC PREPPIES (GREPS)

They've tried pasta primavera, they've tried granola, and they know sushi like I know sushi. Now all they want is pastrami on rye with a pickle from Guss's on Essex. You can recognize them by their favorite old-time songs: "Gimme a Little Knish, Will Ya, Huh?" and "I've Kasha Under My Skin."

People Who Aren't Jewish But You Think They Are Because of Their Names

- Bruce Springsteen
- Henry "Hank" Aaron
- Herschel Walker
- Nancy Walker
- Norman Jewison
- John Steinbeck
- Efrem Zimbalist, Jr.
- George Steinbrenner
- Billy Joel
- Pete Rose
- Steve Allen
- Barry Goldwater
- Aaron Burr
- Ernie and Bert
- John Davidson
- Ringo Starr
- Kevin Kline
- Caspar Weinberger
- Julius Erving
- Valerie Harper
- George M. Cohan
- Whoopi Goldberg
- Benihana
- Julius Caesar
- F. Murray Abraham

Snapshots: High Holy Day Sermons Through the Generations

1940s

"We who have secured the blessings of America would do well to ponder the extraordinary coincidence of Biblical precepts and the principles of the Founding Fathers. Truly, within our tradition can be found the key to realizing the American Dream."

1950s

"As Jews and as Moderns we have enjoyed the blessings brought to us by a successful blending of Biblical precepts and the industrial power of the free enterprise system. Truly, within our system of faith can be found the strength and principles for fighting off the Godless Communists who would shatter our American Dream."

1960s

"We who enjoy the blessings of prosperity cannot stand idly by while the Biblical precepts of peace and justice are violated by those who would deny civil rights on the basis of skin color or self-determination to the noble Southeast Asian. Truly, within our prophetic tradition is the last hope of rescuing the American Dream."

1970s

"As Jews we have always said, 'If I am not for myself, who will be for me?' The Biblical precepts of self-respect before the Holy One are in full consonance with the raised consciousness of the self-actualized American. Truly, within our proud tradition is the emphasis on individual achievement which is the essence of the American Dream."

1980s

"If Moses were alive today, he might be driving a Volvo. Those sandals on his feet would be Gucci. And instead of two tablets of the Law, they'd be printed out on a Toshiba 321. But he would also realize that we who have secured the blessings of America would do well to ponder the extraordinary coincidence of Biblical precepts and the principles of the Founding Fathers. Truly, within our tradition can be found the key to realizing the American Dream."

FIVE WAYS TO AMUSE YOURSELF IN THE RESTROOM DURING HIGH HOLY DAY SERVICES

1. Label the toilets "dairy only" and "meat only."

2. Make a sign that says "Donated in Honor of Yassir Arafat" and hang it over the toilet.

3. Attach a smoke alarm to the wall of the bathroom so that when people come in to smoke, which they're not supposed to do, the alarm will go off.

4. Unroll about six feet of toilet paper. Insert a note on a slip of paper which says "Present this to the Rabbi for a free gift." Roll up the six feet of toilet paper.

5. Put a sign that says "Rabbi's Study" on a stall.

Yiddish: Secret Language of the International Parent Conspiracy

Documents recovered from archives in eastern Europe indicate that in spite of the natural evolution of Yiddish as the language of the Jewish people, it was never taught to children. Rather, it was used exclusively by adults to frustrate the efforts of children to listen in on their conversations. In fact, evidence seems to indicate that the mass migration of Jews to America was engineered to enable parents to speak Yiddish without the danger of children recognizing words from German, Russian, or Polish.

Typically, the family will be gathered around the dining room table, while the kids are eavesdropping from the children's table (two collapsible bridge tables in the kitchen). As the hilarity builds about Ben-Gurion sneezing into Martin Luther King's bellybutton, Uncle Moe delivers the punchline: "So he says, 'Oh! A gezunt in dein shvartze pupik'!"

The adults convulse with laughter. "What's so funny?" the youngsters ask.

Between peals of laughter, someone gasps, "It doesn't translate!"

People Who Shouldn't Be Jews But We'll Never Get Rid of Them Because of Their Names

- Karl Marx
- Rabbi Baruch Korff
- Judge Julius Hoffman
- Howard Stern
- Howard Cosell
- Henry Kissinger
- Abbie Hoffman

- Roy Cohn
- Norman Mailer
- Meir Kahane
- David Lee Roth
- Barry Manilow
- Ed Koch

A Summer in Israel

Some are inspired by the Zionist dream to be a free people in our own land. Some are enthralled by the image of a nation of Davids standing up to the armies of Goliath. Some are moved by the realization of age-old religious aspirations. And some hope the kid will forget about Kathleen while he's there. They all send their children on a pilgrimage to the Holy Land—and the new experts all return with advice for you, which they will offer, unsolicited, the minute you mention you are thinking of going.

Never mind them. *This* stuff is true.

Are there any helpful terms to know?

FELAFEL (feh-LA-fl)
A popular Israeli food made from fried ground chickpeas. The name of this delicacy comes from the fact that after you eat one purchased from a roadside stand, you feel-awful. Other Israeli foods include vegetables, fruit, chicken, vegetables, fruit, and chicken. In some communities in Israel, vegetables, fruit, and chicken are also popular.

HUMOUS (HOO-moose)

A popular Israeli food made from unfried ground chickpeas (notice a pattern?). No food in Israel causes more confusion because it is often spelled creatively in English. One restaurant in Jerusalem advertises that it serves Homos, which has changed the nature of the clientele since the growth of Gay Lib. Another offers you Humus with your meal, and unless you are familiar with this variant spelling, you are likely to expect decayed leaves as a side dish (and those are Greek, not Israeli). Even the standard spelling has been misread as "humorous," leading the uninitiated tourist to expect a floor show, or at least a waiter who used to work at the Second Avenue Deli. *Caveat emptor.*

FOOL (FOOL)

Pine nuts, served as a garnish on Humous. If your waiter spits this word at you when you order Humous, it is neither an editorial comment nor his Mr. T impersonation. Try it, you'll like it.

KIBBUTZ (kee-BOOTS)

A collective farm settlement where socialist principles guide farming and industry. Tractors, furnishings, and spouses are all communal property, except if it is a religious kibbutz, where Jewish law restricts the sharing of spouses who are ritually impure.

CHAVAL (kha-VAL)

An expression which, depending on how it is used, can mean "I'm so sorry" or "Tough cookies." For example, say to an Israeli, "I had a relative who died in a terrorist attack," and he will say, *"Chaval."* Or, say to the clerk at the Jerusalem Plaza, "Leona Helmsley would never issue such thin towels," and he will say, *"Chaval."*

Is it dangerous?

A summer in Israel is no more dangerous than a summer in New York City. As long as you stay inside a locked room, nothing can happen to you. Unless you get blown up.

Do I need to take toilet paper?

Only if you plan to use the toilet while you are there. Unless you get blown up.

Do I need shots?

No, they'll shoot at you when you get there. Unless you get blown up.

How much money will I need?

In the words of a Tel Aviv cab driver we once met, "How much you got?"

What should I bring as gifts for family in Israel?

We used to recommend linens and jeans and calculators, items unavailable except at great expense. Now, however, with the changes in Israel's economy, it is better to give unmarked bills.

Will I meet any important people?

Unquestionably. Stop the first middle-aged man you meet on the street and ask him what he did in the Six Day War. Chances are he will be the first soldier to have liberated Jerusalem. Find a man in his late twenties and ask him about Lebanon. He will tell you he singlehandedly foiled a PLO terrorist attack on the Galilee. Ask anyone over the age of sixty what they remember about the War of Independence and chances are it will be the *very person* who engineered the King David Hotel incident. That's the exciting thing about Israel—there is a hero on every corner.

Can you explain how the system of government works?

It doesn't.

People Who Ought to Be Jews
But Aren't—But We Can Hope

- Alan Alda
- Sally Ride
- Bruce Springsteen
- Bill Cosby
- Mario Cuomo
- Sandra Day O'Connor
- Kurt Vonnegut, Jr.
- Walter Cronkite
- Phil Donahue
- Bishop Tutu (longshot)
- Sen. Daniel Moynihan
- Lee Iacocca

NUMBERS
GRADE POINT AVERAGES, BANK ACCOUNTS, AND TV CHANNELS

How to Choose a College and What to Do When You Get There

The fact of the matter is that you can get a good education no matter where you go to college, as long as you apply yourself and meet the right alumni. It is also possible to go to some fancy-shmancy Ivy League school and, given the right amount of cash and the address of a term-paper research service, never learn a thing. Choosing a school should therefore depend on a number of different factors, including:

1. Where can I get in?
2. What's the Jewish population of the campus?
3. How many Jewish students are from Long Island?
4. Does the school have a law and/or medical library?
5. What is the drinking age in the state?

1. Where can I get in?

This is not quite as important as many people think. After all, lots of people don't get into Harvard. Lots of people don't get into Drake. Some people don't even get into Oakland Community College, but it hasn't stopped them from getting a good education. The key is to pick your ideal school and back up your application with the next best thing.

2. What's the Jewish population of the campus?

This is a crucial question for those out to meet the NJB or NJG (Nice Jewish Boy or Nice Jewish Girl). On the one hand, you don't want to go to some school where there are so few Jews that your arrival on campus is followed within minutes by a visit from the president of the local Temple, asking if you can teach Hebrew School. These colleges are easily identified. Beware if the admissions officer asks during your interview if you are "of the Hebrew persuasion," if the word "Bible" appears in either the name or the motto of the college, or if the college is named for a geographic sector of the state, and then says "state," for those who don't understand that it is a state school. For example, you can bet that there aren't very many Jews at Eastern Wyoming State University or Southern North Dakota State College.

On the other hand, you don't want to move into a ghetto. Chances are that's what you are moving *out* of. Avoid colleges with Hebrew words in their names. It's a safe bet that Talmud Torah University is not going to provide you with cross-cultural experiences that will broaden your horizons.

The best schools to investigate are large state universities in states with large Jewish populations, liberal church-connected universities (Methodist is best), schools near good skiing, any reputable school in the Sun Belt with Miami in its name. (*Caution*: Miami of Ohio is *not* in Florida. Unfortunately, many students, especially those from Cleveland, do not discover this important piece of information until fall midterm time.)

3. How many Jewish students are from Long Island?

If you grew up on the Island, the higher the percentage of people from the same geographic area, the better for you. You won't have to explain your accent, fewer people will tell you they didn't know there were white people in Nassau, and you can share memories of Jones Beach, the Westbury Music Festival, the Islanders, and Fortunoff's.

If you grew up anywhere else, set an absolute maximum number of people from Long Island you will accept among the Jewish population, and eliminate any college which goes beyond your limit.

We recommend a limit of six.

4. Does the school have a law and/or medical library?

The answer to this question must be yes. Always remember the maxim passed down from generation to generation of mothers to daughters: "Always study in the law or medical library."

Similarly, always remember the maxim passed down from generation to generation of senior men to freshman boys: "Always study in the law or medical library. And keep a stack of law or medical books on the desk you use."

5. What is the drinking age in the state?

This question has far-reaching implications. For example, suppose you are very observant of Shabbat, and need to celebrate each Friday night with a glass of wine. Or, suppose you wish to have a Purim party and fulfill the tradition of drinking to excess, made so popular by Hassidim in college towns. Or, suppose you are an alcoholic. Check it out.

When in doubt:
Apply to Brandeis.

Judaism and Computers:
The Prophetic Link-Up

New research has indicated that the invention and applications of the home personal computer were anticipated by the Bible and Jewish tradition. Ancient clues in the sacred books of the Jews, plus a startling piece of tangible evidence, cast new light on the theory that ancient Middle-Eastern civilization was actually visited by an authorized IBM representative.

Item: Matzah is the exact size of a floppy disk.

Item: The earliest story of civilization concerns the introduction of the Apple, which revolutionized society. Years later, the Bible recounts the trials and tribulation of a man named (Steven) Job(s).

Item: The initials IBM can stand for Isaac's Bar Mitzvah, indicating what Abraham gave his son to celebrate his becoming a man.

Item: God spoke to the Israelites from atop Mount Sinai in the voice of a RAM's horn.

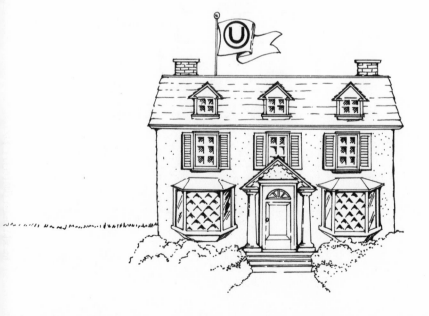

By far, the most convincing piece of evidence is the result of startling research done at Tel Aviv University. Professor Moti Yumat and his team have inserted randomly purchased matzahs into the disk drive of home computers, producing the following schematic of this natural software:

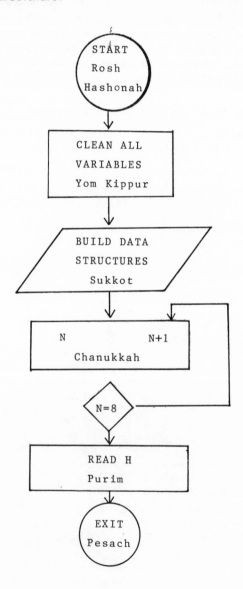

TOP TEN JEWISH BESTSELLERS

THE TALLIS MAN Stephen King
A man is possessed by his prayer shawl.

I'M OKAY, YOU'RE NOT SO AI-AI-AI Thomas Harris
A practical guide to Transactional Guilt.

THE LITTLE PISHER Antoine de Saint-Exupéry
The adventures of a precocious four-year-old Talmudist.

MACBETH SHOLOM William Shakespeare
A rabbi driven to desperation when his contract isn't renewed.

MOBY SHVANTZ Herman Melville
A venereal disease researcher finds symbolism in a whale hunt.

IVANHOEROWITZ Sir Walter Scott
A courageous accountant saves his lady love.

COMMON SEIKHEL Thomas Paine
The manifesto of the American Revolution which gave us the rallying cry: "Think in Yiddish—Dump the British!"

THE GREPS OF WRATH John Steinbeck
A classic of gastronomic revenge, provided the inspiration for Nora Ephron's *Heartburn*.

ALL QUIET ON THE WESTERN WALL Erich Maria Remarque
A young boy falls asleep on the Temple Mount.

THE EXERCIST William Peter Blatty
A suburban housewife is possessed by the spirit of an aerobics instructor, and only her Rabbi can save her.

Jewish Parents Rate the Professions

A recent poll conducted by the public relations firm of Skila, Serefa, Hereg, and Chenek has yielded the first definitive study of parental preferences for their children's occupations. A representative sampling of 10,000 Jewish families with college-bound children was utilized, and the professions were rated according to the Menorah Scale, a system in which nine branches was considered the Ultimate *Kvell* and one branch was considered Irreversible *Plotz*.

Doctor
Attorney
Inventor of Sweet-n-Low

New car sales
Chef
Rabbi

Stockbroker
Medical researcher
CEO of corporation

Used car sales
Sexual dysfunction researcher
Cantor

Entrepreneur (own money)
Diamond merchant
TV anchor

Taxi driver
Cook
Hebrew school principal

Microchip designer
Systems analyst
Movie director

Entrepreneur (parents' money)
Arbitrageur
Bar mitzvah tutor

*Pro baseball player
*Pro football player
*Pro hockey player
**Parent of my grandchildren

Landlord
Jeweler
Retail

---

*No rating. Only laughter recorded on this question.

**Rating exceeds computer capacity.

If Jews Ran the Television Networks

<u>THURSDAY 9:00 P.M.</u>

2 MOVIE: DARK SHABBES (1981)—Thriller
A crazed Hassid uses a timer to cut off the electricity in a Conservative synagogue on a Friday night and holds all the worshippers hostage until they agree to install a *mechitzah* (separation between men and women). Cast: Mendlovich: Bruce Dern; Rabbi Stein: Ed Asner; Mrs. Schwartz: Elizabeth Taylor; Aaron: Robbie Benson. (Made for TV)

4 LITTLE SHUL ON THE PRAIRIE—Drama
Nellie decides to convert, so Mrs. Olson accuses Percival of the blood libel. Pa: Michael Landon; Nellie: Heather Locklear; Percival: Stanley Myron Handelman; Mrs. Olson: Vanessa Redgrave. (1 hour)

7 TWELVE'S COMPANY—Comedy
Jack complains that his two-bedroom apartment is too crowded, so the Rebbe tells him to buy a goat and a chicken and move them in. Jack: John Rubenstein; Rebbe: Burl Ives; Yenta: Bea Arthur. (30 minutes)

11 TWILIGHT ZONE—Suspense
A man gets caught in the Twilight Zone and can't decide between *mincha* (afternoon prayers) and *maariv* (evening prayers). Lieberman: Edward G. Robinson. (30 minutes—Repeat)

20 $64,000 PLEDGE—Game show
Contestants compete for the honor of dedicating a plaque with their name on it over the entrance to the new Jewish Community Center in Far Rockaway or Van Nuys. Host: Monty Hall; Celebrities: Linda Lavin, Soupy Sales. (30 minutes)

<u>THURSDAY 9:30 P.M.</u>

7 CHEERS—Comedy
The new owner, Menachem, wants to change the name of the bar to *L'Chaim*. Menachem: Billy Crystal; Diane: Suzanne Somers; Carla: Rhea Perlman. (30 minutes)

11 DONA, DONA REED—Comedy
Dona spies a calf with a mournful eye on a wagon bound for market, and seeks out Rabbi Judah for help. Dona: Donna Reed; Rabbi Judah: Carl Betz; Calf: Elsie the Cow. (30 minutes—Repeat)

20 $100,000 PYRAMID—Game Show
Hosts: Sam the Sham and the Pharoahs. (30 minutes)

<u>THURSDAY 10:00 P.M.</u>

4 DYNASTY—Drama
The Rebbe is depressed because he has no son to take over the Hassidic sect; Shlomie wants to change his name to Sean and become an actor; a rival sect plans to slip bacon into the synagogue kitchen. Rebbe: Kirk Douglas; Shlomie: Michael Douglas; Rebbitzen: Joan Collins. (1 hour)

7 EIGHT IS NOT ENOUGH—Family
Abbie is pregnant—again—and is afraid to tell Jacob. Abbie: Carol

73

Burnett; Jacob: Harvey Korman; Seymour: Emmanuel Lewis. (1 hour—Repeat)

11 INQUISITION—Talk Show
Hosts Ferdinand and Isabella quiz Spanish Jews about their lifestyles. Featuring Torquemada and his Music Machine. (1 hour)

20 MIAMI WEISS—Crime Drama
An aging New York City police detective retires to southern Florida and investigates crimes against old people. Tonight: Weiss busts a fence who handles stolen gold stars. Weiss: Lou Jacobi; Horowitz: Martin Balsam; Leroy: Eric Laneuville; Gonzalez: Gregory Sierra. (1 hour)

In honor of the birth of our

18 MAZEL NACHAS 18

A 3140257
AUGUST 13, 1987

JOSHUA BENJAMIN

grandpa Ruben
grandma Becky

FIRST GRANDCHILD

Do the Jews Control the Banks?

No, they do not.

If Jews controlled the banks, their influence would be more easily identified. First of all, banks would not be named Chase Manhattan or Continental Illinois. They would be named House of Gelt or Manny, Moe, and Jack—the Loan Arrangers. Second, since the Torah forbids the lending of money at usurous interest, the prime would be down to zero before you could say Federal Reserve Board. And finally, there is the matter of money. If Jews controlled whose pictures went on coins and bills, you can be sure they would find a way to use that power to eliminate the national debt. You want a coin with your picture on it? Perhaps you will dedicate a trade deficit with Japan. Your son's picture on the twenty? Maybe you will underwrite the Department of Housing and Urban Development. You'd like the hundred to honor the memory of your beloved grandparents? There is the matter of grain subsidies for the Soviet Union. After all, dead presidents are all right, but no one ever collected a bequest from Thomas Jefferson.

Do the Jews Control Congress?

For years, anti-Semites have accused Jews of controlling Congress, and for years it has been denied. Ironically, as of 1984 the Jews do control Congress. A recent survey of the 435 representatives has shown that 219 are practicing Jews. Interestingly, twelve members of the Black Congressional Caucus are Ethiopian Jews. On the Senate side, an astounding 62 of the 100 senators identify themselves as Jews.

In spite of the majority of Jews in Congress, the least effective influence on Congress is the so-called Israel lobby. Appropriations to the State of Israel are so high because all sixty-two senators have responded to UJA appeals with the cliché, "I gave at the office," and then realized it was a matter of public record.

Having an Affair
(A WEDDING! SHAME ON YOU FOR THINKING ANYTHING ELSE)

There are six items necessary to make a Jewish wedding a Jewish wedding:

1. A *CHUPA* (the wedding canopy under which the ceremony takes place)
Remember the Cone of Silence from *Get Smart*? That's what the *chupa* is. Anyone standing underneath it cannot be heard—not by those outside, not by those underneath. In this way, the Rabbi can fully discharge his duty to tell the couple the truth about marriage without scaring them off. That truth is contained in . . .

2. THE *KETUBAH* (the marriage contract)
Written in ancient Aramaic, the *ketubah* spells out the relationship between husband and wife. After some perfunctory information, like the names of the participants, the date of the wedding, and the location of the ceremony, the document continues:

> . . . the groom promises to revere, adore, feed, and support the bride in a manner appropriate for a daughter of Israel, and to do so truthfully and faithfully, to provide her bride-price, to feed, clothe, sustain, and have relations with her in the expected manner. The bride, in turn, agrees to turn over her dowry to him, to dress nicely, to live with him, and to share a bed with him and him alone. In consideration, the groom guarantees a sum of 200 zuz.

Of course, the question is, "How much is 200 zuz?" Well, in the popular song *"Chad Gadya,"* the goat is bought for 2 zuz, making 200 zuz the price of 100 goats, enough to make a flock, which is why so many men will claim after divorce that they got fleeced.

3. WINE
To be authentic, the wine must be kosher and thick enough to be mistaken for ketchup. Only the bride and groom drink from the two cups of wine. Everyone else prefers to wait for the good stuff.

4. A GLASS TO BREAK
This ancient custom has been given many meanings, from a reminder of the destruction of the Temple to a bawdy representation of the bride's virginity. Today, many items are substituted for the glass, including light bulbs, small mirrors, and test tubes. Do not use a household tumbler, unless you have among your guests an orthopedic surgeon.

5. *YARMULKES*
It doesn't matter if you are ultra-Orthodox or completely assimilated, you must provide your guests with skullcaps with the names of the bride and groom and the date printed in gold letters. Choose a color that almost coordinates with the wedding colors, but not quite.

Yarmulke collections are an important part of Jewish tradition. It is rare to find a home without a supply of mismatched *yarmulkes* bearing the names of people no one can remember. In fact, when buying a used car, a quick way to check if the previous owner was Jewish is to look for the *yarmulkes* in the glove compartment.

6. AN OLD LADY
If you are lucky, one of the grandmothers will fill this role. Otherwise, someone should be hired to utter the required exhortations.

You also need a band, on which full information can be found in the Bar Mitzvah section.

Finally, bear in mind that Jewish law states that a wedding takes precedence over a funeral, though this custom is often waived if the principal players in each are the same.

An important note to the bride and groom:

Everyone keeps telling you "This is your day." Ignore them. Your job is to show up sober, look good, and get cake pushed in your face. Outside of that, nobody really cares what you think about the wedding plans, so don't fight it.

Oh, there will be those who will tell you they had control of planning their own weddings. Press them for details. You'll find out what they mean is they got the band to play a favorite song, or the Rabbi to agree to wear a yarmulke which coordinated with the gowns. Weddings are for mothers, so if you want to plan one, bide your time and have a daughter. If you want to enjoy one, go to someone else's.

Hair: Now Let's Get This Straight

It seems it is never in fashion. Somehow when everyone is wearing long, straight hair, yours is wavy; and when everyone is wearing those tightly curled styles, yours is wavy. Somewhere between the Middle East and the Old Country the gene pool got polluted with a dominant strain of Permanent Wave DNA.

There are several ways to attack the problem, but all of them have a common enemy: humidity. Like unseen radiation leaking from a nuclear power station, this insidious terrorist to the tresses insinuates its way into your hair and releases the captive wave, often undoing hours of agonizing treatment. Nevertheless, the effort goes on, and short of moving to Death Valley, only these methods have been proven in the War Against the Frizz.

THE HOME CURL RELAXER KIT

Buy the kit in a drugstore. Lock yourself in the bathroom with a window or the smell will kill you. If you are lucky, your hair will come out wimpy and limpy. If you aren't so lucky, your hair will fall out. Have a supply of bandannas on hand to cover your head, and you can pretend to be *frum*.

THE WINTER SOLUTION

Pull a wool stocking cap or ski mask over your head for a few hours on a cold, crisp day. It will mat down your hair in a semblance of cold, crisp lines for the afternoon, as long as you stay in a dry place. *Caution:* Not only will the slightest hint of humidity return your hair to its previous arthritic expression, but your head will smell like your socks.

THE WRAP

Wet your hair, and taking it a section at a time, wrap it tightly around your head so that you look like a mummy. Keep your eyes and nose clear, though you may want to cover your mouth as an aid to dieting. Fasten the hair in place with bobby pins and let it dry—about two days. Hair will come out nice and straight except for the little bumps where the bobby pins were.

THE CAN

Wet your hair and pull it tightly into a ponytail at the top of your head. It should be so tight that your eyebrows can't move. Depending on the length of your hair, wrap it around an empty coffee, vegetable, or orange-juice can. Purists prefer an empty can of Tab. Fasten the hair with bobby pins. Sleep this way, though you'll have to sleep with your eyes open since your ponytail is pulled so tight. In the morning, the hair on the outside will be straight and dry. The hair next to the can will be damp and smell slightly of rust. The ponytail rubber band will leave a permanent ridge in your hair.

THE IRON

This is the classic, time-honored treatment, steeped in the tradition of community because it requires three people: the victim, the person doing the ironing, and the friend to answer the phone while this is all going on. Spread out the hair on an ironing board and press it. Though some recommend the steam setting on the iron, it is dangerously close to humidity, and not advisable. Iron hair right up to the roots or it will have little ridges sprouting. Starch is not recommended.

There is some solace for those who grew up suffering. Your *goyishe* friends with the straight blonde hair will complain about spending $100 on a perm. You can make sympathetic noises on the outside, but, as you learned from The Wrap, what goes around comes around.

What Jews Aren't Afraid of
from A to Z

Arab armies

Buying wholesale

Catholic priests

Doctors

Eating

Florida

Graduate school

Hunting accidents

Israel Bond drives

Jews moving into the
neighborhood

Kennedy, Edward

Lamaze classes

Mastercard

New York City

Orthodontia

Politics

Questions

Rabbis

Saccharin

Technology

United States going to war
against Israel

Violin lessons

Welfare cuts

Xmas tree fires

Yoga

ZPG

What Jews Are Afraid of
from A to Z

Anti-Semitism

Black neighborhoods

Cults

Dogs

Evangelism

Furriers going on strike

Germs

Helms, Jesse

Intermarriage

Jerry Falwell

K-Mart

Lox shortages

Moslem extremists

Nazis

Oral surgery

Pogroms

Quitting school

Rev. Jerry Falwell

Selling arms to Arab nations

Terrorists

United Jewish Appeal fundraisers

Volvo recalls

Wyoming, being transferred to

X-ray therapy

Yom Kippur falling on the last game of the World Series

Zoftig, being called

How a Jewish Teenager Sees Her Nose . . .

. . . and How Her Boyfriend Sees It

"Why Did You Become a Doctor?"

GOYISH	JEWISH

Pediatrician

Dr. K., Boston, MA
"At my first communion, I heard a voice say, 'Suffer the little children unto me.' The inspiration never left me."

Dr. G., Westport, CT
"When I was six, a voice told me I was going to be a doctor. It was my mother's voice, as a matter of fact."

Urologist

Dr. V., Chicago, IL
"I was inspired by my uncle, a pioneer in the field of renal dialysis."

Dr. S., Cleveland, OH
"I was inspired by my uncle, the *mohel*. I always wondered what he really did to me."

General Practitioner—Free Clinic

Dr. A., Detroit, MI
"I was too tall to be Mother Teresa."

Dr. H., Los Angeles, CA
"I was too short to play pro basketball."

Gastroenterologist

Dr. F., New Orleans, LA
"Frankly, I rebelled against my father. He was a gas station attendant all his life."

Dr. W., San Francisco, CA
"Actually, I rebelled against my father. He was a malpractice attorney."

Psychiatrist

Dr. L., New York, NY
"I wasn't called to the priesthood."

Dr. M., New York, NY
"Doctors earn more than rabbis."

The Concise Guide to
Black–Jewish Relations

Do Jews consider Blacks their friends or nemeses? No other question has so occupied the pages of publications devoted to Jewish Existential Angst than this one, with the possible exception of Israel's latest diplomatic blunder. There is no one answer to this puzzle because Jewish-Black relations are not a matter of politics, philosophy, or theology, but of physical proximity:

- Ethiopian Jews are "our reclaimed brothers and sisters"
- Blacks in South Africa are "the noble Africans"
- Civil rights activists are "struggling Black Americans"
- The guy who wants to buy the house next door is "colored"
- The woman who cleans the house is a *"shvartze"*

Simple.

Obstacles to Conversion

The incidence of intermarriage has reached a new high in modern America, and with it comes the problem of conversion. Conversion to Judaism has never been unusual, but there are great obstacles to it today that have nothing to do with ritual and family pressure. The problems arise when two people from strong cultural backgrounds have to deal with:

THE DIFFERENCES

CATHOLIC	JEWISH
God	
Trinity	Unity
Sin	
Guilty until confession makes innocent	Innocent until made to feel guilty
Peculiar Clergy Practices	
Funny clothes Celibacy	Funny hats Atrocious sense of humor
Highest Earthly Authority	
The Pope	An uncle who keeps kosher
Meaning of Christmas	
"Joy to the world, The Lord is come..."	"Irv, how much longer do we have to play 'Joy to the World' over the Muzak system?"
Sex	
Only when necessary for children	Fully endorsed

Church/Synagogue Affiliation

Fully endorsed   Only when necessary for
                                  children

Favorite Dead Language

Latin   Hebrew

Evidence of Resurrection

Easter   Hebrew

Pride and Joy

John F. Kennedy   Albert Einstein

What to Do with an Unleavened Wafer

Take communion   Have a seder

Most Common Middle Name Which Is Never Used as a First Name Because Any Kid with a First Name Like This Would Die of Embarrassment

Xavier   Mendl

What You Go to Talk to a Clergyman About Even Though If You Thought About It First You'd Realize That *He* Knows Less Than *You*

Marriage   Interfaith dating

What You Are Expected to Letter in During High School

Football   Debate

Organ Most Likely to Succumb to the Ravages of Lifestyle

Liver   Heart

Strange Bedfellows:
Religions and Politics

Through the years Jews of all persuasions have been active in American politics, and this has brought us into consonance and conflict with members of other faiths. For a long time, there was no way to tell if the topic of conversation was going to lead to brotherhood or blows, but decades of discussion have led to this handy guide to the mainline stances of major denominations on the hot issues of our time. If you find yourself in an interfaith situation, like a meeting of the National Conference of Christians and Jews, an office cocktail party, or a wedding, simply choose a topic designed to promote either good will or good debate.

KEY: C = Catholics   P = Protestants   E = Evangelicals
S = Secular humanists*

AGREEMENT	DISAGREEMENT
Abortion	
P, S	C, E
"Star Wars"	
C, P, S	E
Israel	
E	C, P, S
School Prayer	
P, S	C, E
In Vitro Fertilization	
P, S, E	C
Euthanasia	
C, P, E	S
How to Make a Corned Beef Sandwich	
	C, P, E, S

*Classified as a religion even though most secular humanists swear to God it isn't.

The Secrets of Long Life

For countless generations, the ancients have passed down to the young the secrets of long life. Gathered here, for the first time, are the only formulas proven effective after centuries of research, presented by their leading proponents:

Ida Shvartzman, 93. Solomon the Wise Nursing Home and Mortuary, Lakewood, NJ.
"Don't die."

Sidney Nussbaum, 94. C/O Katz's Delicatessen, Fairfax, Los Angeles, CA.
"Every morning, get up."

Selma Kogan, 88. Winston Towers, West Rogers Park, Chicago, IL.
"Pretend to be much older than you really are."

Nate Goodman, 79. Crown Hotel, Miami Beach, FL.
"If you eat herring for a hundred years, you'll live a long time."

Lev Gorowitz, 85. Formerly of Moscow, USSR; currently of Brooklyn, NY.
"Move to the Soviet Union and become a dissident. Dissidents in the USSR never die of old age."

Bessie Katzoff, 86. Anshei Aztec Retirement Village, Phoenix, AZ.
"Never completely pay off your pledge to the UJA."

ACKNOWLEDGMENTS

The following people deserve a lot of credit for all the help they have provided:

Howard Zaharoff contributed his Yuppie Haggadah, Qumran Parchment, and holiday insights, as well as sundry suggestions and one-liners. He is the funniest lawyer I never met. Ann Moline, my wife, contributed the section on hair (the hair piece?), her laughter and criticism, her encouragement and support and a lot of great ideas. She is wonderful beyond words. Richard Moline, my brother, contributed pieces on summer camp and Israel, as well as feedback on all the material. Rabbi Jim Michaels contributed the piece on Hebrew School. Rick Dinitz contributed the computer flow chart. Barbra Eventov contributed the idea for the circumcision illustration. Eugene Davidson, my father-in-law, lent me his computer to make my work so much easier and gave me the story about his grandfather's wedding night advice.

Lots of others went out of their way to help with ideas, and their influence is felt throughout the book. My parents, Herb and Dolly Moline, Joni Crounse, Carol Davidson, Cheryl Rosenthal, Robert Golenbock, Michael Kaufmann, Julie Moline, Arthur Lavinsky, and Andrew Kurtzman all have my deepest gratitude. I also appreciate the patience and affection of Congregation B'nai Israel of Danbury, Connecticut, which served as sounding board for this material.

Thanks also go to Mindy Werner, a great editor; Ginny Rubel, a great designer; and my agents and friends, Madeleine Morel and Karen Moline (who also contributed the piece on chicken).

Finally, but most importantly, my thanks to my illustrator, Marcia Simha, whose name I found in the Yellow Pages and whose humor and talent are a reflection of her name.

PENGUIN BOOKS
GROWING UP JEWISH

Jack Moline, Rabbi of Congregation B'nai Israel, Danbury, Connecticut, is a graduate of the Jewish Theological Seminary in New York and Northwestern University School of Speech. His articles have appeared in numerous publications, including *Sh'ma* and *Moment* magazines, and he has served as Resolutions Chairman for the Rabbinical Assembly. Rabbi Moline lives in Danbury, Connecticut with his wife Ann and their two daughters, Jennie and Julia.